THE WHITE HOUSE

WASHINGTON

July 10, 1991

Dear Dr. Chadha:

Thank you for your thoughtful letter and for enclosing a copy of your book, The Other Side of Golf. I appreciate this special remembrance and your kind words.

Best wishes.

Sincerely,

Dr. Jaideep Singh Chadha
SCF-18
Sector 8-B
Chandigarh
INDIA

by the same author

PLEASE MOM! IT'S MY LIFE

The funny side of GOLF

Revised Edition

Dr. Jaideep Singh Chadha

J-3/16 , Daryaganj, New Delhi-110002
☎ 23276539, 23272783, 23272784 • *Fax:* 011-23260518
E-mail: info@pustakmahal.com • *Website:* www.pustakmahal.com

London Office
5, Roddell Court, Bath Road, Slough SL3 OQJ, England
E-mail: pustakmahaluk@pustakmahal.com

Sales Centre
10-B, Netaji Subhash Marg, Daryaganj, New Delhi-110002
☎ 23268292, 23268293, 23279900 • *Fax:* 011-23280567
E-mail: rapidexdelhi@indiatimes.com

Branch Offices
Bangalore: ☎ 22234025
E-mail: pmblr@sancharnet.in • pustak@sancharnet.in
Mumbai: ☎ 22010941
E-mail: rapidex@bom5.vsnl.net.in
Patna: ☎ 3294193 • *Telefax:* 0612-2302719
E-mail: rapidexptn@rediffmail.com
Hyderabad: *Telefax:* 040-24737290
E-mail: pustakmahalhyd@yahoo.co.in

Earlier this book printed under the title—
The Other Side of Golf

ISBN 978-81-223-0947-8

Edition : 2007

Printed at : Param Offsetters, Okhla, New Delhi-110020

Contents

Preface to the Revised Edition

I am indebted to two special people, President George Bush, for his letter of acknowledgement written at a time when he was busy trying to pry out the Iraqis from the sand bunkers of Kuwait and to the one and only Mr. Khushwant Singh, for his review, where he wrote that President Bush could not have had the time to read the book at all! Since he is a golfer himself, he should know about the desperation of truly determined hackers which forces them to read up all available literature, just to improve their game. But this point can be debated with considerable verve and fury at the 19th hole (hic!). Till it is proved either way, we shall let it rest.

I would also like to clarify that this book was never meant to be a joke book. The jokes that are in it are only for the younger golfers, to be used in moments of stress. They are not mine and are definitely not new. In fact, I am envious of those who have been on the golf course long enough to have heard them all. I belong to a generation that came along much later and had a whale of a time laughing my guts out when I heard them for the first time. I also managed to do some wild hitting as a consequence. Anyway, the primary role of the book was to tell the perpetrators that their activities are known to all and sundry; also to laugh and make life a little easier to live.

After observing many more golfers from the observatory of a golfing doctor's mind, I have collected valuable data and incorporated it into the revised edition. I hope it helps the younger players to become better golfers.

Special thanks go out to Charlie, who should be 86 now. He made these beautiful cartoons.

Introduction

I have flared up at many a party, for I was confused and thus angry. The reason was not earth-shattering. It was in relation to golf. No, I wasn't angry at golf itself. How could I be? I have always been a sportsman. To me, golf was just a game, like any other. I was angry with those who played golf with their tongues instead of golf clubs—at parties! I was angry at their inability to read the bored-to-death expressions of their audiences. What bugged me more was the consistency of their behaviour.

I decided to figure out the hows and whys. How does the golf club imbibe this egoistic trait into men the world over—almost instantaneously—the moment they hold on to one? Or is it the ball? I thought about my own days when I played competitive badminton. In those days, I was considered something of an artist. I could hit the shuttle at any angle I wanted; a flick of my wrist would send the opponent jerking and shunting all over the court, except where the shuttle finally landed, that is. My spin serve would get him into all kinds of mental and physical troubles, my drops would sail through the air and land on to the net and, half-heartedly, tumble over to the opponent's court, almost in slow motion. But never have I sat down to discuss with anyone at a party about how well I played or dropped or sliced or smashed. Neither did my friends.

Then how do we explain the behaviour of golfers? Could it be that one rarely comes across a person who played badminton at that level? Could be. Or is that in every elite gathering, almost everybody plays golf or at least is supposed to? But the answer still eluded me. So I decided to join the gang to find out what makes them tick. I met golfers and saw them playing. Till now, I had dubbed golf a 'talker's game' and you know why. What I discovered was pretty simple. Most regular players were mediocre and played for the sake of enjoying the game and the camaraderie that it involved. I rarely saw the party golfers on the course. The real players, with handicaps ranging between four and fifteen, were the silent ones. Some of them were even embarrassed talking about their prowess with the golf club and what they could do to the ball with it. For them, the orgasmic ecstasy of hitting the ball right was enough.

I was then scared. I wondered what the future held for me. Would I become the talking golfer, or the playing golfer? And if I did become a talking golfer, I wondered what I would talk about! After all, there are only the clubs and the balls! Oh yes! and the greens, the handicaps, the pars, the hole in ones and the course. Ah! and the swing, and the putt!

I went after golf like a race dog goes after a rabbit. This game continued to fool me even when I thought I was good. Despite the fact that I had brought down my handicap down to eight in a hurry and played in the "Chandigarh WILL'S Open" held in 1989, I still sliced when I shouldn't have, topped balls, missed putts, duffed sure winners, went into roughs a thousand times, lost balls and did things which humiliate me to this day. I have even had nightmares because of the ball lying in a divot. I played with golfers who did everything I did and a lot more. But they seemed contented with their handicaps. There was another difference. They won most of the time. I noticed people hit perfect greeners from difficult fairway bunkers, from under low shrubs, never lost balls and as a result, never lost.

Thus, I decided to delve deeper into their *modus operandi* and succeeded in unearthing new techniques of golf. It was these very people who gave me lectures about golf being a gentleman's game. I agreed with them whole-heartedly and decided to educate other gentlemen through *this book.* Readers can pick and choose from *The funny side of Golf* and win—every time!

Happy Golfing!

(author)
jaichadha2001@yahoo.co.in

Classification of Golfers

The first job that I had on hand was to know the people involved with the game of golf. The ones who played themselves, and the ones who had bum chums who played but had never been on the course themselves. Then I decided to give my well researched advice to both groups of golfers so that they would come out winners, on or off the course!

The Fantasisers

Definition: These are cerebral golfers, for the only course that they have any sort of contact with is in their head, and in any case, the only golf that they have played is mental. Their initiation to golf is through idle talk at parties where golfers usually dominate the scene and play collective lingual golf.

If you fall into this category, don't lose heart. There is no harm in being a golf fantasiser. If the bug has bitten you theoretically, and you feel a strange emptiness gnaw at your insides when you are supposed to be having a good time at parties, just because you cannot be an active participant in golfing dialogues being thrown at you, then, read on, very carefully.

First of all, you simply must learn a few standard golf phrases, e.g. "So, how's golfing?" Or "How is the game treating you?" "Handicap down to single figure

19
BLAB
BLAB
BLAB

yet?" Or "Still trying to hit the ball out of sight?" Terms like slicing, chipping and drawing, pitch–n–run, grainy greens, club head speed and other technicalities should roll off your tongue with precision and dispatch. Everything about the swing, in all it's glory, should be learnt from a person who can actually play golf. Because this is what the golfer is perpetually worrying about. The swing could be "Out-to-in" on one day and then suddenly change course and become "In-to-out" the next day. He might generate a professional swing today and then moan the next day that he has no idea what a swing should be. Hence, there is no need to be as confused as the run-of-the-mill, garden variety golfer. Just take some professional advice yourself, so that you can help out these poor guys.

Please tread with extreme caution when making a point of reference to the term 'slice'. Remember, the word is poison. If you ask a golfer about his slice, it is like hitting him below the belt when he is not looking. Turn into an unassailable authority about golfing equipment and pros. For example, you should know about the various golf sets that are available, their past, current and future prices, the superiority of stiff over regular shafts and the age groups that should use them, types thereof, i.e. steel, titanium, boron graphite and whatever else golf scientists and golf magazines can keep throwing up at this game from time to time. And while you are at it, look up the importance of grooves on the club head. The most over-ruling aspect of it all is your ability to throw the vast store of knowledge that you have in your arsenal, back at the lingual golfer, with a poker face as if you have been doing this all your life and are the

unparalleled archetype for the disbursement of condescending advice to a nincompoopial gathering.

You can open the argument implicating trousers, insisting that they are the most wretched articles of golfing attire ever designed. After all, the Scots did play golf in their beloved 'kilts' not worrying about appearances. The Pakistanis tried to improve upon them by inventing the 'salwar kameez', which is better, but far from perfect. It does provide a comfortable knee bend, so essential for a good posture at address, but the kameez hinders in the swing. Moreover, which man worth his manhood wants to look like a woman anyway. But, Indians are different. We are so good at aping the West that we tend to forget our own goodies in the good old 'dhoti'. They performed exceptionally in almost every activity when they had it on. Even during the Satyagraha. If one goes back in time, even the Mahabharata was fought in dhotis (and because of them too, if you remember how the story goes), against the mighty Ravana, the dhoti proved most sturdy also. If only Indian golfers had an open mind on the issue, they would realise that the dhoti is the best thing going for a good, unhindered knee bend and a smooth waist turn, resulting in a perfect swing.

If someone in your audience begins to sway, sweat or faint at the thought of being seen in a dhoti, you can begin your defence and marketing of the dhoti in earnest. Tell them about **it's adjustable sex appeal and how well it fits into the sexually orientated scenario of golf just by exposing only so much 'leg' as one considers sexy.** Tell them about the variety of material the dhoti offers. These days, jute is so much in vogue. One can wear coloured, printed or just plain jute. We can have an exaggerated sex appeal by staying with the original translucent malmal. It could trigger a riot of imagination. If one really wants to flaunt his cash in style, silk dhotis would to the trick. Don't forget the woollen ones for winters. Tell them about the regional style of tying the dhoti.

If someone in the gathering airs an opinion about how time consuming a dhoti tying operation could be, just say, "Wake up, baby! This is the new age. If complicated nappies have been revolutionised with the discovery of the disposable ones with Velcro, why can't we take a leaf out of their book and come out with ready to wear dhotis, Velcro and all?

Dhritrashtra, the blind king, had a hundred sons even when he used the conventional dhoti. If there had been dhotis with Velcro in those days, can you imagine what the Kaurava population would have been? The Pandavas could barely handle the hundred Kaurava Princes and had to muster the guile and cunning of Krishna to do them in!

Contempory headgear could be improved upon with a 'Gandhi topi' in any material with nationalistic slogans splattered on the sides. Some suggested slogans are:

- Kill two birds with one stone: use khadi or jute condoms.
- Sleep on nail beds for foolproof family planning. India needs your sacrifice.
- Help Indian P & T. Write more letters. It doesn't matter to whom.
- Help Indian Railways. Travel more. It really doesn't matter where.

- Sing patriotic songs... all the time.

Or, one could always bring a new "I love....." series on the same lines.

Indians haven't made it to the international scene because of their poor playing standard. But the dhoti and the Gandhi topi can get prime coverage on ESPN They will take the golfing world by storm!!!

I am sure your listeners have, by now, got a shell-shocked expression on their faces. Their mental computers would be working overtime wondering how they are going to sell their line of golfing attire to Pierre Cardin.

One important thing that you could do would be to breeze through some of the mail order catalogues while you are perched on the "Throne" early in the morning, and memorise a few names of the world's top pros. Because, quite a few golf sets and balls are named after them. Then comes the never-ending topic of balls. Your core knowledge of Balatas, dimples in all shapes and configuration and what they do to balls and their performance is essential. An in-depth knowledge of golf shoes and the importance of leathers vis-a-vis rubbers, especially in the Indian context, and Jungle boots in winters, and all because they are both so hardy—the shoes and the Punjabis, that is, never mind the greens which are being literally raped. The Captain and the green keeper are there just to clean up after the Jungle boots have done their bit. Thus, explaining to your rapt listeners why FJ's are superior to the rest of them put together might not prove to be such an easy task, at least in this part of the country. Do not forget paraphernalia like visors, gloves, T-shirts, belts etc. Once you know about a few of these things, I can't promise you a PhD in Golfeology, but I can certainly assure livelier parties, where you will be the centre of attraction. Golfing friends will be flabbergasted and will wonder where and how you acquired such prodigious knowledge of the game without ever slicing a ball.

As a parting shot, just ask them to look around for a good set for you, preferably a boron graphite Mizuno. If someone catches you on the wrong foot and conjures one up, you can always wriggle out of that one by saying that there is no 'feel'. Remember, so much in golf depends upon the 'feel'! If you don't have 'it' then you have nothing.

The Most Popular Golfer

This is the guy who is or at least thinks he is, the most popular golfer on the course. He can be recognised from a mile and a half. He usually has a 'fixed' grin on his face as he goes around saying his 'Good mornings', 'Salam waleykums' and 'Satsriakals' dutifully to every passing member, his shadow, his children, caddies, gardeners, the security staff and the waiters. After some time, his smile gets grooved like a pro's swing. He even starts to "Hi Tiger" the course mongrels, lolling in the sand bunkers, forgetting that tigers in the sand are bound to screw some unfortunate golfer's bunker shot. As he goes around the club house in a trance, with his right arm raised in a perpetual salute to people in and out of sight, he hears calls of "Hi Balraj! How about a game at 1.30 this Saturday?" Since he has already taken the word 'No' out of his vocabulary, how can the most popular one say 'NO'!?

By the time he has taken a round of the course, the Gazebo, the club house, the bar, toilets, changing rooms and locker rooms, looking for people who might acknowledge him, he has already confirmed eleven people for 1.30 on Saturday, the 25th of December!

The scenario on the first tee on Saturday is typical. Our most popular one, armed with his deadly smile and his mighty boron teflon graphite, Super Jumbo

GOOD MORNING ?
GOOD MORNING

driver, descends on to the first tee like a pleasanter version of Changez Khan, out to conquer the world by his goodness and sunny personality. It suddenly dawns upon him that there are eleven people looking up at him with great expectation and oops……! He realises why, but the exalted one doesn't get fazed one bit by the chorus "Hi Balraj, all set?" emanating from eleven different throats. This one is a doer. So he immediately sets things right by making three four balls and nominating a Round Robin tournament. Thus, an exhilarating round of golf comes to a successful conclusion, thanks to our hero of the course.

But this guy is often late because of so many pressing engagements. Sometimes he misses out on his original four ball that have teed off in the hope that he will catch them on the short third. But then, there is another three ball waiting for a fourth and they consider themselves very lucky when they spot Balraj hurrying down. Everything goes very smoothly, till around the fourth, when a shout of "Hey Balraj! You ditcher!" bifurcates the fairways, splintering the silence on the course. Mind you, this is his original four ball pining for him, calling out from across the seven seas. Balraj knows what to do. He stops his swing midway, bestows his new partners with deadly smiles, hands his club back to his caddy, and says, "Thanks a lot folks. Duty calls. Nice playing with you." And off he goes to join his originals.

He has completely failed to notice the open mouthed, F-16 lamblasted expression of wonder spanning the faces of the three golfers upon whom destiny has descended with such nerve-shattering force. One moment they are the envy of the whole club after bagging the most popular one and in the very next, they are stripped of all—everything and sundry. Their esteem and ego takes a nosedive, but no one can be annoyed with Balraj for very long. After all, how else would he be the most popular one?

One important aspect of our hero is that he scrutinises everything with his X-ray vision. He keeps an eye on golfers playing on the course and if someone has an errant ball in the rough, our man flint will tell them which blade of grass it is lying next to. He will also tell him what was wrong with his swing when he hit the ball into the rough. When he gets back to the club house, he will hand over the list of articles littering the course to the Assistant Secretary or to the President, if he is around.

God bless the most popular one and his purse when, on the 19th, he keeps telling the waiter, "Un sahib ko ek large drink lagao." And may they keep flowing....

Grouch on the Course

You can be a grouch anywhere—in the office, school, or hospital, but if you happen to be a golfer too, then you have to be a super grouch. This man is totally allergic to the rule book. He is a great admirer of Italian driving, the rear view mirrors are a source of annoyance to him. His visits to the course will be without his rear view mirror. So if you have ambitions in the realm of the grouch, you must follow rules of your own. Some of the accepted ones are as follows:

- Never annoy your regular four ball regularly.
- You must greet one or two new golfers with great courtesy everyday. In addition, there

should be phases where you should be on your best behaviour. This helps in keeping people on their toes and always wondering about your motives. They will, as a result, be unsure of what is expected of them. Thus, it is the driver's seat for you always. You can alternate between a good guy on one day and a grouch on the next, depending upon the situation and your mood.

- You must criticise almost everything. If there are red flowers blooming on the first tee, you must criticise the Captain for his poor taste. Doesn't he know that the colour red is a sexually oriented one? As it is golf is a very sexual game, what with golfer's talking about clubs, balls and holes all the time. The red colour plays havoc with the mind of the golfer on the very first tee. They should plant blue coloured flowers on the first tee and save the red ones for the last holes.
- Always reject the first caddy allotted to you. This keeps the second one alert.
- Check what is not on the day's menu at the Gazebo and then ask for it specially. This gives you an opportunity to criticise the chairman of the catering committee.
- If the greens have been covered with top soil, shout like hell when you miss your putt. If it hasn't been covered, then you can always growl about unkempt greens.
- Be very finicky about giving a pass. If you are a genuinely slow four ball, and if you intend handing out passes like they distribute condoms

in Thailand, then you had better carry sleeping bags with you, for I can visualise you on the courses for an eternity. In any case, how can one be a grouch and allow people through too? Remember, you have dispensed with the rear view mirror! A pro grouch should be like a wall between the ones behind you and the next green. You should have an explanation for all your actions which make you a slow golfer. After all, if you don't take three practice swings, how else are you going to groove your swing. And if you don't practice again and again after missing your original two footer, how else are you going to discover what went wrong with your first putt?

- And if, after hitting your drive, your tee sails off to an unknown destination, aren't you justified in looking for it till the next four ball comes along and offers to carry on the search for you at a later date? After all, tees are an integral part of your golfing paraphernalia, but the good grouch should never provide explanations for his actions. As an effective grouch, if he has to command any respect, he should shun all thoughts of approval. Your actions are only to give happiness to yourself.
- A good grouch always takes the help of his caddy while taking a line. This helps. Because if you putt it, then all credit to you. Otherwise, you have a ready-made scapegoat! Never ask your partner for the line. This way he can't act superior.

If you are one of those religious golfers who must pray before every shot, where is the harm? Just that trait qualifies you to sainthood. People should be thrilled at the sanctity that you bring with you to the course. Agreed that it does slow you up a little, but that is no reason to give a pass to mere mortals. And if you have arthritis or say, angina, and you have an interrupted gait? So, what happens then? It could happen to anyone, even to the ones who are clamouring for a pass. How does it matter to anyone if the green ahead of you is vacant. Does it get bored? Or has it been ordained that all holes on the course have to be busy all the time? And then, grouch or no grouch, hurry also takes time.

If you are a grouch who can play good golf and are a fast player too, then life is made. You can exercise your vocal cords too, and in the bargain get maximum satiation out of the situation. So what if your shouting makes the whole course jittery enough to miss putts and duff shots all the way. The orgasmic ecstasy the whole exercise provides to you is worth all that and more.

And if you have read "Your Erroneous Zones," you should have understood by now that you have been fed with too many 'shoulds' in your life. For example, you should play fast, or you should wear spiked shoes or you should repair your divots and pitch marks. Dr. Dyer advises that one should ignore the 'should dos' of our life and do things which give us true enjoyment. Why do anything that the golf etiquette book tells us to do? One must play golf in the manner which gives 'us,' the grouches, the greatest pleasure. Only then can one be a true grouch on the courses.

Finally, when the true grouch has finished his round of enjoyable golf (even if he was the only one who enjoyed it) and the time has come to pay the caddy, say he doesn't deserve a farthing, for he did not have his horoscope for the day with him, and neither did he visit the temple before coming to the golf club. That is why you missed so many putts. He gave so many wrong lines and handed wrong clubs all the time!!

Grouch Hits Someone with Ball

They say that the chances of hitting the other guy with a ball are very rare—say around 1:10,000. That is the good news. You want to believe it with all your heart. But the bad news is that you happen to hit the guy twice on the same day and that too on the same hole.

Even with luck like yours, there is hope. Chances are that the guy you hit did not actually see you hit him on either occasion. OK. This is one moment when you should keep your wits very near, in a handy location. The left cerebral hemisphere would do every well for starters. This small incident should be treated exactly like a roadside accident. If you have any experience in that region, then it helps a lot. But if you don't, then just go on reading. It does not matter which school of scruples you belong to. This is neither the time nor the place to practice the good ones.

Quickly drop another ball of the same number and make, and hit it out to the side opposite to where your injured golfing friend lies groaning, holding on

to whichever part of his anatomy that you hit. Then take off towards the second ball after a loud "Shit, a duck hook", if you have to go to the left, (or "Oh, not another shank", if you have to go to the right) as if you are completely unaware of the calamity that has befallen your friend. By and by, your attention will veer towards the four caddies and two golfers who have collected around the groaner. And everyone will see you walk towards them from the opposite side of the fairway. But in real life, such things rarely happen. Even if no one else has seen you floor the poor guy, the course mongrel will have seen you do the honours. He is bound to give you away. Remember, if there is a dog around the accident site, you are certain to be caught. Because dogs have a strange, happy kind of sadness around them, like the aura of a holy man. You will be the sad one here, when it barks your secret away. So keep all dogs at bay.

The caddy's silence can be bought. Just a wink helps. But if the poor chap was watching you hit the ball with his legs crossed, but was too slow to move out of the way, then you will have to say a small 'Sorry' to him, because the ball misbehaved. But remember, never apologise in public. For you might have to deny your very existence on the course that day if he lodges a complaint against you at a later date. So once he is in a better frame of mind, steer him away from the others and whisper whatever you have to say in his ear, just like they do in the confession pen. Invite him to the 19th hole for a drink in the evening, with the sole intention of getting him sozzled enough to forget the existence of that fateful day itself.

But a true grouch would ideally lamblast the golfer for not being more careful. After all, it is his responsibility for the well-being of his own head. How can you be answerable for things which have so many variables? The club head can open or close at the last moment. It can raise it's head and top the ball which, while departing in a lower trajectory, fail to clear the other fellow's head.

Strokes

A good grouch should argue with his four ball over strokes on the 1st tee—even if he plays everyday, with the same guys. Your handicapping should be like the Argentinian price index. It should change every hour. If your four ball refuses to give you enough strokes, be a good grouch and announce, "OK! In that case, there is no sense in playing with you guys. I am leaving!" and walk off the tee. Can you imagine what will happen to the other three? They will be on their knees and give you what you want.

Advice for the Soon-to-be-Married Golfers

If you are in the marriageable age group, warn your parents that they should never sit and brag about the love that their ward has for the game of golf. There have been instances where the girl in question or the girls' mother have refused an otherwise perfect match just because the groom-to-be turned out to be good golfer. So, if you are asked by the other party about your association with the game, act as if you did not know that it was a game. All along you had thought that golf was an abbreviation, which stood for:

G GERIATRIC
O ORGANISATION OF THE
L LAME AND
F FEEBLE

You should make it very obvious that you don't feel sheepish but almost a sheep because of this complete lack of general knowledge.

The Newly Married Golfer

So, it has been a happy ending or should I say beginning. If you have been accepted despite your

mother bragging about your golfing prowess, then I say you are very lucky. So let's keep it that way.

Obviously, the cute little thing that you married will want to participate in every activity that you indulge in. That means she wants to learn the game of golf. That decision should normally be described as catastrophic. But then you are lucky. You have me telling you what to do.

The first thing that you have to do is to *look* absolutely thrilled that your newly-found one and only wants to play your beloved game. Act as if the stars have come out with sunshine in your life. Ecstasy should be the expression for the coming days. Ask your beloved to go and buy herself a full golf kit. The best should include trousers, T-shirts, visors, golf shoes, gloves and the half golf socks. You should hire a ladies' golf set.

Practice balls can be bought from the pro shop. Everything is set for the lady to learn golf. Set an appointment with your local pro. Never teach her yourself because of two reasons. First, you will lose your own golfing time with your buddies and second, when she hits air shots repeatedly or when the ball travels two and a half feet with the accompanied squeals of delight, it is bound to get you riled up. Hence, no need to get upset. Just let the club pro suffer.

Suddenly, you might find your collection of balls missing from the refrigerator. On enquiry, you might be told ever so sweetly that the old practice balls hardly travel! These new balls are much better. You instantly think about the dozen or so balls of Titliest Pro V that you were saving for special games. And

Balls missing from the refrigerator.

the cost!!! But then you can't be squeamish where your beloved is concerned. And that too for a short time.

When you go out for a round and you spot her on the practice area, jog up to her and see if everything is fine. Make sure she has her bottle of nimbu pani, her napkins and the suntan lotion. Peck her on the left cheek and off you go. You can now take that breath you were holding on to.

And then the day arrives when she has to go for her first round on the course. You know that it is going to be one long round for the club pro. So start them off early. 6 a.m. should do very well. Two things will happen. She will enter the 10 o'clock morning sun, miss her lunch and then she will again miss going into the shade. That means a round of about 8 hours punctuated by the many passes she has had to give to the four balls behind her, who have grown old waiting for her to somehow reach the greens. By the time she comes back, you will almost let a shriek escape from your sealed lips. Who wants to see his newly-found tanned!? Hearing your shriek, she will run to the ladies' room and you will hear another shriek. Which newly-wed, in her senses, wants to be tanned!? It should be more of the FAIR AND LOVELY!

You should be waiting outside her door and catch the pearly-eyed look. Believe me, she would be looking lovely despite the tan. You can almost anticipate the next dialogue. It should be "Darling! I really don't know how you do it everyday! I tried, for your sake, so that we could be together on the course! But it seems like it is a game that makes a person very tired!

And look what it did to my complexion! And I have been saving it for you for years!"

Don't be in a hurry to show your happiness. Hide your glee till she is out of sight. See, all your sacrifices paid off. With interest. Now she must be feeling very guilty for letting you down. No way is she ever going to blame you for playing this game called GOLF!

How to Win at Golf .... Every time

There are two oft-quoted statements associated with golf. First, that golf is a gentleman's game and second, that it is all in the mind. I agree with the second. It is the attitude which makes you play well or disastrously. To win, you must think positive. Contrarily, the first quote is bullshit, a figment of imagination, bubbling out of a defeatist mind. All games are played by 'gentlemen'! It is these gentlemen who kick the other 'gentleman's' ball out of the field. Only gentlemen in hockey splinter the other guy's shin with their hockey sticks and again only gentlemen crack open skulls with a cricket ball! Even an athlete will try to trip the chappy who is trying to overtake him. Mind you, he too is a pucca gentleman. They do this only to win. I do not include boxers into this category, for their *modus operandi* is a bit different. Don't get me wrong—I am not asking you to take out your iron and beat the shit out of your opponent. But there are other ways to win in golf.....every time!

It is the club pro who brainwashes every golfer with such crap. Let's get away from such morbid thoughts which shackle the imagination and limit our capabilities. At some stage in the course of the game, it ceases to remain just that. It turns into war. Since everything is fair in love, war and games, let's get on with the winning aspect.

Choosing your Partner

Having the right man as your ally is most important. Let luck rest on the back seat for a change. Be aggressive and take the opportunity to throw balls for partners. You know who is the better player, so hold back his ball along with yours in the last three fingers as you throw them over your head. Most likely the balls held together will stay together. As with everything in life, this being an art form too, requires a lot of practice. Once you know that you have the capability to pick and choose your partner, your confidence will get a great boost, for half the battle is won if you have a good partner.

OK! If your ball gets a kick to the right or to the left, or if it gets a back spin or a top spin, and the intended balls get separated, don't let that small thing get you into a fit. So what if the guy you were calling a prick becomes your partner. He now becomes a 'gentleman prick.' Golf being such a complicated game, it also gives you a couple of hundred acres to operate in or almost an eight and a half kilometre zone as the sizzled crow flies, to plan your opponent-destroying strategies!

Setting up the Handicaps

This is one point during strategic warfare where losing an argument is plain and uncomplicated suicide. So, argue like hell. Praise your opponents to heaven and back. Write poetry about their orgasmic drives, their accurate iron play which probably could put Tiger Woods to shame, their ability to hole from miles, their excellent putting, even if they miss three inch putts on a regular basis. Never forget to tell them about the lousy game that you play. Tell that to forget your 9 handicap on the board. It was a punishment handicap for not filling in enough cards. And in any case, that was ages back, most likely in your previous birth! Tell them what an atrocious player your partner is—he would miss a six inch putt even if the hole was as wide as a well. Ignore the sidelong murderous glances that your partner is trying to lance you with. It can be explained to him later. If your opponent has also read this book, then it all boils down to the sustaining power in your vocal cords.

Opening Drive on the First Tee

I presume that you have won the skirmishes of the handicap and that you have a partner of your choice. That simply means that you have very magnanimously given the honour to your opponent and that he has to drive first. What happens on the first tee will determine the course of the entire game. As he surveys the scene ahead of him, take some wild swings which miss his head by inches. Since that is the only head that he has, he will be adequately shaken. There are some golfers who lose their tempers very very quickly. He will give you one of those 'if-looks-could-kill' stares and say "Do you mind? Someone is trying to play golf here."

Forget niceties like 'Sorry'. They just weaken your resolve to win. So just keep quiet. Sometimes, silence does more damage than shouting back.

Goebbels would have called this 'disinformation' and so would I. Don't go around coining fancy names like 'deceit' for what you have to do next. Wet your middle finger with your saliva, exactly like the shippies, and raise it to the breeze and say, "Shit! It is right to left breeze!" (actually it is a head-on wind). Please note that small expletives like 'bloody shit', 'holy cow', have a great demoralising effect on your opponents. Despite the fact that he has already noted that it is a head-on wind in the first place, he will still pluck some grass and throw it into the wind. It will most naturally come back and whip him in the face. Don't get rattled. Say "Jeez! The wind sure is on a ball today! We will have to be careful today."

If the previous forecast did not upset him, the ominous wind behaviour will.

Your opponent is finally set to whack the ball to kingdom come. Notice how he glares at the ball and then at some vague spot on the fairway. His glare oscillates between the ball and the green. This is hypnotism. God only knows whom he wants to hypnotise. But your job is to break that spell. Just ask him some innocuous question. Ask him if he holds his breath during the swing. Notice how he stiffens immediately. It is so obvious that he has never paid any attention to this vital aspect of a good, smooth swing. After some practice swings, he will answer 'Yes' or 'No', as the case might be. If it is in the affirmative, ask him if he does that on the upswing or the downswing. Whatever his answer, just shout "HOLY SHIT" on the upswing (or downswing). Rustle up the worst smirk that you can and sock it to him.

After that, just clam up and look up at the sky with the most bored expression that you can produce. It should silently scream "Mama Mia!! Imagine playing with a guy who holds his breath on the upswing," (or downswing as the case might be)! As if that is the most important thing in the world of golf. The effect of the wind factor and the breath-holding will be twofold. Firstly, he will try to adjust his swing according to the swirling wind that you so kindly informed him about and secondly, thinking about the breath-holding, he will viciously slice his ball into the out-of-bounds.

Not only this, if you look at his partner, he too would be swinging away to glory and his forehead will be furrowed with frowns as wide and as deep as the SYL canal and its tributaries. He too will be worried about what happens to his breath during his backswing and downswing.

Net Result: You have just destroyed their drives for the next seventeen holes. By now, dreams of jogging all the way to the bank should have just surfaced.

When it is your turn to drive, take your time. Tee up your ball, go behind it and analyse the line, direction and the height of the ball. Suddenly, you don't like it. It seems half an mm too high. Take your driver and carefully tap the ball which will further tap the tee and it will pierce the ground only half an mm. Mind you, not many people can tap the ball without letting it fall off the tee. Remember, everyone is watching. Then take four perfect practice swings—absolute slow take away, pause for 20 milliseconds on the top of your swing and then a perfect downswing along with the finest weight shift that there is. Remember, every amateur can make the most perfect empty swing. Tiger Woods would turn green watching you swing. After your follow through, hold your pose like good old Gavaskar.* Then stare at the ground. Suddenly, you don't like the area. Pull out your tee and replace it after you have levelled it with your shoe and then with your driver.

Quote Jack Nicklaus: "Nicklaus bhaji says that golf is already a difficult game. Don't make it more difficult by choosing an uneven ground for your tee shots," and laugh loudly. Begin your practice swing routine again and then hit a nice and easy drive which will naturally bifurcate the fairway. Any hapless trees in the way will be too ashamed to be standing in your path and will sway to one side. If your tee jumps four feet backwards, say, "See, a typical Nicklaus bhaji shot!" Finally, jog off the tee!

The Faithfuls

Then there are some golfers who think that they *have* to show their devotion to the Lord above. They will sky the ball fairly regularly. These are the 'Faithfuls'. All you are supposed to say is, "Ah! The 'OH-GOD-I-AM-COMING' shot!" Then go on and tell them the 'Oh-God' joke.

Ten-year-old Tom asks his mother, "Mother, why does our maid Anne want to go to God?"

---

*Gavaskar: Legendary Indian Cricketer.

The mother says, "No, child! Anne doesn't want to go to God."

The child is adamant, "Oh yes, she does! I saw Dad trying to hold her down on the kitchen floor while she was screaming, "Oh, God! I am coming! I am coming!"

The unexpected: Your opponent might be made of a special metal if your practice swings, the disinformation, or the psychological warfare about his swing did not affect him. What should you do then?

Remedy: Tell him some sick jokes.

(i) **Jack hits a dream shot. Jason, his opponent, asks him, "Are you in the bunker my friend, or are you on the green, you bastard?" Then laugh like mad. The other guy has to laugh out of politeness. Have you ever seen a guy hit a dream shot when his body is shaking?**

(ii) **A lady standing near the eighteenth hole, while waiting for her husband, gets fascinated by another golfer walking up. Every time he puts his right leg forward, there is a big bulge which comes on with it. As he comes abreast, she cannot hold her curiosity any longer. "Excuse me, Sir," she says, "but is something wrong there?" The approaching golfer has two golf balls in his right pocket. He has had a bad round and is not in a mood for long dialogues. To**

> **cut things short, he says, "Oh, I have golf balls." The lady is intrigued, "You mean like athlete's foot, and tennis elbow, you have golf balls?"**

Don't wait for his reaction. Have a good laugh yourself. Better still—guffaw! I am sure our objective has been reached—metal notwithstanding.

Bad Lies and Some Remedies

A good caddy is worth his weight in gold. He will remove your ball from a divot. If the ball is lying behind a big tree, he will remove the tree for you. He will drop your ball in a safe place if you happen to be in the 'Out-of-Bounds'. But sometimes, a clever opponent will get your caddy marked. Now, it is all up to you. When the ball is under a low shrub, or in a fairway bunker, use the tee liberally to tee up the ball. Then send the blighter screaming to the green, much to your opponent's chagrin. Don't forget to retrieve your tee to avoid embarrassment later. If your ball gets lost, never let that worry you. A hole in the pocket is the greatest invention since pink condoms. A ball of the same number and colour may be dropped at a convenient location. Mind you, this little deception can be played up by your opponent too. If you suspect your opponent of indulging in this sort of a thing, and he yells, "I've got it" as you reach the green, then drastic action should be taken. Instruct your caddy to press his ball into the ground the next time he drops into the rough. Then camouflage it with leaves. When he yells, "I've found it" as you reach the green, your caddy should retrieve it. Pat the caddie's head and confront your opponent with, "I wonder whose ball this is." If he denies any relationship with it, then you are richer by a ball. In addition, you have given him a subtle hint that you are in the know, and that your

Remedies for bad lies.

hair hasn't turned grey in the sun for nothing. If your ball gets caught in roughs like the ones you come across in the Delhi Golf Club, where there is a thick overgrowth of trees, ask your caddy to hurl the ball out in true Azharuddin* under-arm style while you hit out an imaginary ball.

Then yell like mad, "Anyone see my ball come out?" They most certainly will have! One should always help out the partner. After all, what are partners for? If he is looking for his ball in the tall grass, and if you find it first, just pick it up, put it in your pocket and drop it in a clear space using that hole you have there. Then shout, "Partner! You were looking in the wrong place. Here it is!" Similarly, if your opponent goes into the rough, go on in yourself and pretend searching for it. It pays to be helpful here.

When he does find it, stand on his head as he addresses it. Even if he doesn't move the ball say, "Sorry, but you moved it. That is one stroke gone." Naturally, he will vehemently object and say, "NO! I did NOT!" Shrug your shoulders and say "Okay." But that minor loss of concentration should goad him on to duff his shot. Even your presence will psyche him to hit the solitary twig in his path.

Things get really exciting as one reaches the periphery of the green. Try to reach the green before your opponent. Even if it is his honour to hit, just ignore him and hit your shot first. Once he sees you near the pin, he will be under pressure to do better than that or at least come near. You know what people do

---

*Azharuddin: India's ace batsman and former captain of the Indian Cricket Team.

under pressure. Either they play better golf or like most golfers, they wilt. Advantage to you, my friend.

Usually, there are a lot of trees around greens. There was a guy I saw rustle up an arse swivelling act. At first I really did not catch on. It seemed as if he had an itch you know where. I manoeuvred myself into a good vantage position. He had the ball between his feet and when he was sure no one was looking, he would swivel his backside sideways so that when he straightened out, he was six inches from where he was standing. In ten deftly performed rotations, he had the ball almost out, far from the trees. Since I wasn't part of that four ball, I was just a bit wiser in the art of survival.

As you approach your balls lying on the periphery of the green, concentration is vital. So don't let him concentrate.

Tell him this joke. Or any joke.

Example to Centrifugalize Opponent's Mind with Joke

You know, there was this lady who went to an avid golfer-cum-hunter's lodge and began to look around. She knew about most of the trophies on the walls. She saw deer, lion and buffalo looking down at her. Since she was from the interior of South Africa, she wondered about the small spherical object mounted on a stand. As the hunter came in, she asked him, "John, what is this?" John replied, "Oh, that's a golf ball" (he had won it for a hole-in-one). Now, Jane didn't know what golf was but she knew

that it was better to be considered a fool than to open your mouth and confirm it. So she did not open her mouth. Six months later, she came to the city again and went to see John. Everything else was the same as before, except that next to the first 'golf' ball, there was another 'golf' ball on a small stand (John had another hole-in-one).

This time Jane knew what it was, so she was understandably ecstatic.

"Oh John!" she exclaimed, "You shot ANOTHER GOLF!"

The best way is to make the joke linger, so that it is only half told by the time he reaches his ball. Carry on telling him the joke as he addresses the ball and as he gets ready to hit, say, "Hit your shot first and then I'll finish it."

The fellow's mind will be on Jane and what the golfer did to her in the lodge. How the hell is he going to concentrate? So, when he hits a bad shot, start the joke all over again.

Sometimes you want the guy to get confused. So tell him a confusing joke.

Two drunkards were out on a stroll. They were fairly sentimental by then. The first fellow says to fellow drunkard, "Say, Harry! Who do you think is your right hand. Harry?"

"My wife ish my right hand," says Harry.

First fellow: "And when your wife is not there, then?"

Harry: "Oh! Then my right hand ish my right hand."

Your opponent is likely to be confused because he'll wonder what you are talking about. Is the right hand the right hand because it is important or...why? Don't forget to laugh and show your superior sense of humour, even if he does not laugh.

Another Confusing Joke

An avid golfer has a dream of a conversation with God. Naturally, they get to discussing golf. So he says, "God, how about golf courses in heaven?"

God replies, "Son, the whole of Heaven is one big golf course. But there is a bit of good news and there is a bit of news which you might consider to be bad. Which one should I tell you first?"

Golfer, without thinking blurts out, "The good one first please, God."

And God says, "Okay! The good news is that the golf course in Heaven is like Heaven. There are no obstacles, there are no bunkers, and because of the clouds, you get a tremendous divot. There are no trees either. The caddies are all ex-film starlets!"

Golfer gets excited, "Wow! Great! What's the bad news?"

God says, "Son, you are booked on a four ball at 2.57 p.m. next Thursday!"

Or you can irritate him.

Girl meets boy and introduces herself, "Hi! I am Harinder, but Harry to you!"

Boy replies, "Oh! I am Balwinder, but Balls to you!"

"Imagination Tickling" Joke

Harry goes out to play golf alone, on a new course. Every now and then, he forgets which hole he is playing. There is a lady playing ahead of him, (also alone). On the 9th, he asks her, "Excuse me, Madam, which hole are you on?"

"Tenth," she replies. Harry exclaims, "So I must have played the 9th."

On the 15th he asks her again, and she replies "Sixteenth!" and he says "Ah! I must be on the 15th."

On the 17th, he gets to her again and she says, "I have finished the 18th," and he says "Ah! I must have finished the 17th!"

They meet at the bar and he gets talking to her and says "I am Harry," and she says "Jane," and they shake hands.

He asks her if she is a working woman and she says, "Yes. I work for a firm which makes sanitary pads. And you?"

And Harry says, "God! What a coincidence! Here, too, I am one hole behind you. I work for a firm which makes toilet paper!"

Importance of Riddles

In situations where immense quantities of concentration are required, for example, bunker shots with the pin placed just next to the lip, riddles are of paramount importance. Because these will get the opponent's mind entangled into a web of it's own kind; something similar to what the Americans did to President Saddam Hussein. It would be reasonably correct to assume that he must be the world's best sand bunker player with all that sand surrounding him. If George Bush foxed him in that region, it could only have been by riddling Saddam's mind into a spin. I am sure he did not tell him a joke since they had never met before hostilities began. He must have sent him a riddle.

Anyway, one such riddle is as follows

A pencil sharpener was having an affair with two handsome looking pencils. Then the inevitable happens. The sharpener gets pregnant. And there arises a paternity dispute. Which of the two pencils is the father?

Remember, the timing is of great importance. This should be narrated to the opponent as he frets over his second shot landing into the greenside bunker. The narration of the riddle should end the moment he extends his hand for the sand wedge. As he stands, deeply wedged into the sand, contemplating his shot, concentration writ large on his forehead, say **"Think about the answer after completing this shot."** Unknown to his guy, his mind has already gone into a wild spin. And with each passing second, the spin will get wilder, very much like the one you saw in the movie "Twister." Trust me, I know what I am talking about. Soon he won't even be able to focus on the ball. The ball will take the shape of a pencil. Rather, he will be seeing two pencils. Because, technically, his cortex has been divided into two extra layers. One is thinking about the shot, which should have a soft landing, ending three and a half inches from the pin. And just below the first layer, the second will be bubbling for a judgement in the disputed parenthood case.

Great! His partner will only feel the ball whizzing past his head as it lands in the bunker on the opposite side. He doesn't mind the bad shot. What upsets him more will be the complete lack of emotion on his partner's facial screen for hitting a shot of that kind. Because any golfer worth his salt, never mind his handicap, is acutely embarrassed after a bunker-to-bunker shot of that kind. On the other hand, he will be confused about the funny expression on his partner's face—as if he is trying to solve a riddle (he doesn't know about the riddle, yet). Meanwhile, the recently appointed judge will give up after spoiling a few more shots and call out from across the fairway, **"OK, so which one is it?"**

You can now safely call back, **"THE ONE WITHOUT THE RUBBER!!!"**

And then there are the supposed to be real life riddles for the feeble minded golfers.

A religious nurse, who was having an affair with a doctor, gets pregnant. Her religious beliefs prevent her from going in for an abortion. So the ovum turns into a foetus and keeps growing while the parents carry on with their argument. When just a month is left for the foetus to turn into a baby, the jubilant doctor enters the surgery and hugs the nurse who, unfortunately is unable to share his euphoria. The doctor shouts happily, "Darling, I have the perfect solution." The nurse replies somewhat sadly, "Are we not a little late in the day for all that?"

"Don't worry about a thing! The priest is coming in for a prostatectomy next month and I intend to palm the baby off to him."

So, after the operation, the priest asks the doctor, "Son, how did the operation go?" And the surgeon replies, "Like a dream, Father, like a dream. But there was a miracle too. You delivered a baby boy." The priest just nods his head in a knowing manner. The surgeon is astounded by the lack of any surprised reaction from the priest. And after everything is over, the priest carries the baby home. Eighteen years later, the priest, now an old and feeble man, decides to tell the boy the truth, so he calls him into his study and tells him, "Son, I have a confession to make. I am not your father."

The young man is shocked. He says, "And then who is my father?"

The priest replies, "Son, I am your mother. The archbishop is your father."

The bunker should have arrived by now, and your opponent should be asking for his sand wedge any time. I will leave you to your devious tricks.

Value of emotionalism.

One of the most important things in golf is on-the-spot coaching. If you are a steady eighteen to sixteen handicapper, all the better. Because then you enjoy the best of all the worlds there are. You should, as a rule, tell the eight handicapper all you know about the right kind of swing, what he should have done in the last hole, how he should have cut the ball to get more back spin and all that. You have to be a trifle patient with the low handicapper because he will duff shots all right, but not with the same speedy frequency as that of sixteen or eighteen handicappers. That special trait you have of being helpful to society will be brought to its maximum use if your opponent is an inconsistent sixteen. Every time he hits a skier, tell him how he dropped his shoulder too early on, that he lifted his left heel, fell on the back foot like Navjot Singh Sidhu*, used too much force, and so on. If he tops a ball, go haywire with coaching. First tell him he was standing too far, then his butt wasn't out enough, his head went with the swing, first to the right and then to the left, his chin was high up in the air. Show him how it should have been done. Don't show him with your club. Relieve him of his club even if he is reluctant to part with it. Then do it rightly, up to almost perfection. Since there is no ball, you can do a masterly job. Make sure you take two or three solid divots hitting the club hard into the ground.

This will have two effects on him. Firstly, the opponent will wonder where he went wrong, and then he will be angry, because you are misusing his club. Well,

*Siddhu: Well-known Indian Cricketer.

that is the general idea. When it is your turn, and if you have by chance hit a perfect shot on to the green, ten feet from the pin, curse like mad. Use expletives like "Bitch!"

Say "Bitch! I wanted a 2.8 degree fade. The bitch did 3.5." Now get real angry. Hit your club into the ground. Stamp the grass under your feet with all the venom you can muster. Better still, throw your club in such a way that it misses your opponent's partner by the hair on the skin of his Dartos* muscle. Then shout, "Idiot! You come here to play golf. You can't even play ping pong! Go home, you pip-squeak Ajay Pal Singh (if your name is Ajay Pal Singh) and play marbles. Make sure that when you throw your club, it should go forward, down the fairway, not backwards. Otherwise you waste precious energy going back to pick it up. Your opponents will be flabbergasted by your desire for perfection. They will wonder what else you want in life? Hit a Birdie for Chrissakes? After all, you are an eighteen handicapper or thereabouts.

There is another tactic here which works wonders. If you have hit a near perfect shot, you can go overboard with self praise. Make sure that the opponent forgets his own shots as you remind him of what a perfect third shot you had on the fifth. Better still, praise all your shots like mad, even if the grass went further than the ball. You can explain that one away by telling him how you wanted to hit exactly that kind of shot, and did. The green offers you great opportunities and these should be like an airline pilot's checklist which

*Thin muscle covering the testis.

one should follow religiously. If the opponent is ten feet from the pin, one must remind him of the possibility of an 'easy' three putt. Don't mark your ball because as I shall explain later, this tactic has a great future. If you or your partner are somewhere near the green in four and your opponent is on the green in three, announce that you have a fair chance to halve the hole. Your opponent is bound to wonder how that is possible. If he is reasonably intelligent, he will realise that the only way that could happen is if he three putts his eight footer, and you chip and putt. He should always be made to realise that he could either hit a short putt or go six feet over. In all probability, he will do one of the two.

You should announce your opinion of the speed of the green, 'slow', 'fast', 'badly cut' or 'bald!' Even if he has a straight putt, remind him of the difficult line that he will have to take. If he wants to get your ball marked before he putts, then put your marker in front of your ball. When you replace your ball, put it in front on the marker. Two to three inches can be gained every time you putt, and remember, each inch matters.

Things are likely to get too serious for comfort, because your opponent is working up his concentration for the putt. *Break it.* The best way to do it is by a joke. If you are around a bunker, tell him a bunker joke. **You know, in Japan, girls caddy for you. There is this guy who, after hitting a shot, says to his caddy, "I think it is on the edge of the bunker." The caddy politely tells him that it is 'in' the bunker. The golfer is adamant and says, "No. It is on the 'lip' of the bunker." The caddy has lost all patience by then and instead of telling him that he is blind as a bat,**

she says, "Look here. Sir! When a woman tells you it is 'in', it 'IS IN'! And you better believe it!"

Let's suppose that it is your opponent's honour to putt. He bends down to see the terrain on which he is going to putt and finally takes his stance. At that moment, ask him if he would like your ball marked, even if it is lying four feet from his line. He will take his eye off his own ball to tell you that it doesn't matter. Then start taking practice swings with your putter, standing in his line of vision, so that your movements disturb him. If you notice him glaring at you, or if he moves away from his ball, desist, to avoid confrontation. As he prepares to putt, call out to someone (it doesn't matter who), not to move when someone is putting, or bring out a ferocious sounding battle cry, "SSHHUSSH!"

The ability of a golfer to recognise the arrival of a critical moment in a game is the hallmark of a true champion. This gift of God separates the men from the boys. One such moment is when the opponent is all set to putt a two footer for a win. Don't do anything silly like taking practice swings with your driver in an attempt to blow his head off. Neither is it any good to shoo off the rain bird which always wants to know "Did you do it, did you do it, did you do IT?"

What is required here is—finesse! Apply all the honey that the bees have manufactured over the course to your voice, so that when you ask him the fatal question, it is literally dripping honey. Go for the balls, man. Ask him, "How many shots have you had till now? Eight, or is it nine?"

The gullible golfer will straighten up and start counting, "From the tee, my drive went to the ladies' tee, second to the rough, the third went back to the tee after hitting the tree, the fourth landed in the fairway bunker, the fifth was well out, the sixth on the edge of the green, and here I am, all set to put it in, in eight."

Now, enter the ring flailing with both fists. "What about the one which almost went O.B? I think it would be nine in." The gullible golfer will go up to the caddy and ask, "How many hooye?" The caddy will say, "in 8." Glare at the caddy and say, "Count again" even if what he said was God's truth. Suddenly, the course will light up because of the fireworks started by the four ball behind you. They have been waiting almost an eternity for you to finish the hole. Be magnanimous again and say, "Go ahead and putt. We will do the counting later!" In his embarrassed confusion, shame, latent anger and a few other emotions pooled together, he will pull the ball away from the line of the putt.

Then you might come across the egoistic dream golfer. His ego will be so easily and deeply pricked that he will lose his temper before you can say f...! He'll hiss. "I told you it is seven and so, seven it is!" Something in your expression should tell him that you don't believe him. He will explode like an 'amoebic fart'. "Are you, by any remote chance, insinuating that I lie?" That's it! Let him putt in that frame of mind and see the results. The hole is already yours. Guaranteed!

When it is your chance to putt, transform yourself into a pro. Under no circumstances should you walk up to the ball and putt straight off. Psyche the ball from all directions. Examine the turf to see which way it is cut. If you are a Sikh, see which way the wind blows your moustache. Lie down on the green to see which way the ball will turn, bend on one knee like King Arthur proposing, and then finally address the ball. Take as many practice swings as you feel like. Then as you get ready, and everyone is waiting with baited breath, move away from the ball suddenly and vocally lacerate the opponent's caddy. The bigger choice abuses, the better. Tell him if he moves again while you are putting, you will break his head. Go up and address the ball again and putt. If it goes in, all your hard work has paid off. If it doesn't go in, lambast the caddy again for having spoilt your concentration.

If you come to within six inches of the pin after a thirty foot putt, sit down on the green with your head in your hands and moan as if your favourite goldfish has just drowned. The opponent is bound to say "Good putt!" Take it in the sarcastic vein and lament, "In golf, every shot makes someone very happy." And walk off.

Your opponent will be so demoralised at his own lack of perfection that he will strive harder at making a better golfer out of himself. True, one should strive for greater heights in golf (like everything else in life) but that, as a rule, should be done on the practice range and not during a game. So when your opponent commits the blunder of trying to improve and reach your high standards, he would have messed up his game. He will begin by holding the putter hard and then the left hand will take over and pull the putt to the left. Then he will try to emulate your drives and fairway shots by using too much force and happily for you, he will duff more shots than he could ever imagine himself capable of.

Here comes the interesting part. He has by now spoilt so many shots that it is no longer funny. He will wonder why and will begin to look for areas where things usually go wrong, and as you know, in golf, there aren't many. There is only the grip, the square, open or closed stance, the swing, with a slow take away and fast downswing and club head speed. It could be an inside to outside, out to in or an inside to inside swing. Then there is the weight shift, the breaking of the wrist at the right moment, the importance of the left heel, the head movement, the shoulder drop and the force. There are a few other things of lesser importance which he will automatically think about when he takes a swing next time.

At that moment, strange sounds resembling an African dialect will emerge from his cranial cavity because of the stony thoughts rattling in his cranium. After all, the best imitation of Yoruba can be produced by rattling four stones of three inches diameter in an empty Dalda tin, and Ibira, by rattling six such stones in a three-litre motor oil can, half filled with water.

Once this happens, you know that the moment to deliver the *coup de grace* has arrived. This time tell him a medical joke.

The class for that day was on Pediculosis. The demonstrator took out a monster from his hair and said, "Boys and Girls, this is Pediculus capitis, and is very common." After showing it around, he phooed it away. Next, he pulled out another monster from his body and said, "This is called Pediculus corporis. This too is very common." He showed it around and then, like the first variety, phooed it away too. Then he dug into his trousers and after

SAPLING

some searching around brought out a cute little thing. "This," he said in a hushed tone, "is Pediculus pubis, and is very rare!" And lovingly puts it right back.

Another example of a medical joke: **The Professor was explaining an important procedure called the Pre-Rectal examination. He said, "Boys and Girls! This is a very important procedure. It might be painful to the patient, though more to his pride than anything else. While preparing, talk to him about some unrelated subject. You can ask him about his smoking habits, and proceed as I shall presently demonstrate." The professor put on his glove, applied vaseline, asked the patient to lower his pyjamas, turn to the other side so that his back was towards him, and then finally to bend his right leg. The patient did all of this very grudgingly, for the procedure was embarrassing.**

As the professor got ready, he asked the patient, "Baba, do you smoke?" The agitated patient turned around and asked in a surprised tone, "Oh! Is smoke coming out from there too?"

Or tell him a mother-in-law joke:

A golfer takes his cocker spaniel to the vet and says, "Cut off the stump of his tail."

The vet says, "But all that is left of the tail is the stump. Why cut that off?"

The golfer replies, "My mother-in-law is coming to stay with me. I don't want any visible evidence of welcome, for she doesn't like my playing golf!"

One factor which interferes with our winning or losing, is LUCK. So many times, after a good shot, the ball is found languishing in a crater in the thickest rough. Getting out of the rough is hard enough, so who wants craters. We find Lady Luck laughing at us from behind a tree. It is at moments like these that one looks for a hydrogen bomb to blast the tree behind which sniggers Lady Luck. But beware of exposing emotions loosely. Put on a perfectly hard, stone-faced expression, dig into your bag and produce a white marker that they have in 'Saplings'. If the opponent is far away, the caddy can mark the crater. Don't you worry about the astonished expression of your opponent when he says, "Now, why the hell have they put a marker in the middle of nowhere? There is no sapling visible from here to eternity!" He will scratch his head to patchy baldness.

There are some instances where the ground had been under repair. We might feel the GUR boards have been prematurely removed. The ball can find itself in a bald, barren patch. Don't worry, be happy. Just take out one of the GUR boards that you have stashed in your emergency survival kit and dig it in. Naturally you get a drop from such places. Your opponent is bound to say, "What in tarnation is happening around here? Golf rules are changing faster than a chameleon changing colours!"

Occultism in Golf

Most golfers are oblivious of occultism in golf, though all pros are seasoned practitioners of this art. Haven't we heard the pro talking to his ball, "Okay, baby! Do it right the first time. Go straight for a 100 yards and then turn right at an easy curve of 60 degrees. Keep going for another 50 yards and then SIT!" And the ball does just that! To you, he sweetly says, "See, I sliced the ball for a bird."

But you know better now.

Till you mature in this art of the occult as a pro, limit yourself to the green. It is easier and produces instant gratifying results. As your opponent gets ready to putt, just cut his line with your putter or circle the hole with it, intoning some African juju mantra. If you are not well versed with juju, the good old 'Choo mantar, kali kalandar....' will do. The results are astonishing. The ball will stay short of the line, or it will go all around the hole and prefer to stay out. It might race for the hole and then suddenly brake and hover on the edge of the hole. No amount of screaming, pleading or stamping will coax the ball to drop in. It might even surprise you when you hole out even after hitting a way-out putt. Later, as you improve your skill, activity can be extended to the fairways. Balls belonging to the other party will suddenly veer to the left or right, hit trees which they were never even supposed to look at, and land in the 'Out of bounds'. The opponent will find his ball lodged in the deepest recess in the roots of a tree. Your own ball, which was heading straight for the bunker will suddenly turn towards the green and stop next to the flag-pole. A word of caution here. Do not hole out from two hundred yards. That would be cheating. Practice will help you to attain greater heights of occultism in golf.

Medicine and Golf

Contrary to popular lay belief, golf is a very stressful game. That is, if you can call it a game at all. I call it a vocation, a life long dedication to a cause—to balls, clubs and assholes.

In fact, the stress is so omnipresent that there is not a single moment in a hacker's life when he can quit worrying. There is a very intimate three-way relationship between rain, weekends and golf. If one is a weekend golfer, he is bound to start worrying about the weather from Monday morning onwards. Worrying if one will get a game on Saturday or not, is very logical. And if one is in the habit of playing in a fixed four ball, then the itinerary of the other three seems so important. And if all that is set, getting a good time slot for tee off takes the next berth on the worry panel. If every thing goes according to plans, and if one is a resident of Chandigarh, one has to keep praying that no acquaintance dies, because all funerals and bhog ceremonies are usually on prime golfing time.

On the fateful day of the game, as one drives through the gate of the golf club, one begins to worry about getting proper parking space. And if you are the superstitious kind, like I am, then there is nothing to stop one worrying about the caddy that one is going to be allotted, and whether his stars coincide with yours on that day and time. Because that is all that separates you from wining—the caddy's stars, what else?

Finally you are on the first tee, nicely attired for your game, with the watch ticking away towards tee off time. Suddenly, one finds that the others have not arrived. One begins to eye other four balls suspiciously and begins to worry if the starter has missed you out in his list and substituted the fellow who is ominously taking practice swings with four clubs. Once you have verified your tee off status, it is only natural to worry if the four ball ahead of you is the high betting type, who will crawl for the next five hours to complete the round, or if they are the bridge types who will take six hours. And when you have finished worrying about all these matters, your friends will eventually troop in, four and a half minutes to tee off. Then the four of you will worry as if it is four and a half minutes to a nuclear strike. Will I get an air shot on the first tee shot? Everyone is looking, damn it.

But the major issue of stress is yet to come. When you throw balls, who knows if we have had sufficient practice of throwing balls for partners or not. As a consequence, worrying who your partner will be, and if he will succeed in convincing the other party of his fake handicap or not. After all, who likes to have a partner who agrees to play to his actual handicap. No one, not even a cretin would want a guy who plays to sixteen and says his handicap is twelve, just to impress God only knows who, for a partner! Such people should be run out of town the moment such disastrous attitude is known. It is nice to know if one's partner will cheat during the game or not. What is the idea of having a partner, who, in a God forsaken rough with civilisation no where in sight, comes back to confess that his ball moved when a butterfly sitting on top of the ball farted, and as a result, takes a voluntary penalty? Banish such thoughts, please. PLEASE!!!

Our American friends are very used to stress on American soil. But once they are sent to destinations outside America, their stress rises to phenomenal levels. Hence they have psychological therapy sessions for all their employees and their wives. One such man posted in Hong Kong provides a perfect example of their stress level. He was trying to get into a lift as two Chinese nationals were coming out. He could only enter the lift after the two had emerged. This small incident caused him so much stress that he had to go back to his psychologist for therapy. In comparison, normal Indians do not suffer from this malady on Indian or foreign soil. The reason for this aberration was explained away by another American stress expert, through a unique hypothesis. He said that most Indians have a very low AH Factor, (Arse Hole Factor, it does not constrict in moments of stress, as it does in chickens and Americans)!

But Indians golfers are not like other ordinary run-of-the-mill Indian low AH factor. For them the stress is greatest when they address the ball on the first tee, mainly because of the gallery. Moreover, weekenders don't touch their clubs for the whole week. How it will respond to the occasion is something only the result will tell. If their ball decides to fly off in the right direction, all is well, till the second shot lands in the bunkers, of course no gallery awaits them here.

Romantic dialogues will do very well.

Only the stress that they might hit into the sand too heavily, in which case their ball might not move at all, or they might hit the ball directly, resulting in their ball landing in the bunker on the other side. Then comes the stressful thought, "Will I ever reach the green?"

This is roughly the pattern which will carry on through eighteen holes. Will two footer putts be missed? Will the opponent birdie from off the green? When in the rough, will the opponents force the five minutes rule before the ball is found? Did the caddy withhold some vital aspect of his horoscope since things were not going too well? Will he keep on hitting the microscopic twigs in his path? Will trees shift their positions and lean into his ball's flight path? Will his ball suddenly develop some sort of affinity for the out of bounds. Mind you, in golf all this constitutes major stress. Hats off to the Indian low AH factor. Not many people have dropped dead on the course. So, it couldn't be that bad.

All said and done, golf should still be treated like a game and not a career by amateur golfers, especially those in the geriatric age group. One should take out all frustrations of life on the ball. Trust me, I know what I am talking about. The ball is designed just for that purpose. It can take all the shit you can manage to throw at it and it at. So treat it like a true friend. That is exactly what true friends are for. Do what the pros do. Talk to it more often. Confide all your woes to it and see how it absorbs everything.

Coming to the treatment proper, by the time we become senior active members like they have in the Rotary Club, and have been playing golf for many years, the stress, irrespective of our low AH factor, hypertension and ischemic heart disease, must have already taken abode in our system. Just go out and choose a good doctor who will treat your maladies and let you forget about the rest, let golf take it's own course.

Medical Emergencies and the Golf Course

Snakes and Bees

Most golfers have had nightmares involving these creatures on the course or in their dreams. If you have had dreams with snakes playing a dominant role, don't worry. Be happy, for these, according to Freud, are sex symbols (move over Imran Khan) but if they arrive on the scene as you are about to hit a shot in the rough, then it is not all that sexy. The snakes and the bees have a funny notion that they have a territorial right over golf courses and it is golfers who have taken over what is rightly theirs. As you know, reasoning is one of the weaker character traits of both these wonders, hence, one should know the odds that one is battling against.

Snakes

These are otherwise very shy and sensible slitherers on the course. Basically, they realise that golfers are environment friendly people who come back to the course again, again and again, only to dig up the area for future wheat plantation (or any other crop which suits the environment). The only difference lies in the implements that the golfers use for digging and

Sssnakezz.....

harvesting. They hack at the vegetation instead of cutting. And they use a small ball as an excuse.

The problems arise only when one annoys these fellows by stepping on tails. Waiting and wondering if the snake belongs to the 10% poisonous minority or the 90% non poisonous majority serves no purpose and is fraught with the risk of the fellow giving you a tiny nick on your nearest anatomy. Trying to kill takes too much time and chances are that you might not even succeed in that venture at the end of it all, and end up on the losing side. After all, hitting a moving snake with the club head while you are shaking all over, is a difficult task. I don't recommend heroics of any sort.

Just run for it like mad. Any direction will do, as far as it takes you away from that area, for there might be more of its kind lurking nearby. Sometimes, one does get nicked. Prayer, they say, helps more than panic, and head for the nearest doctor or hospital.

Bees

These are mighty unfriendly creatures. Their behaviour towards golfers can be attributed to their dislike for movement as they stage their fly-past (exactly like some of our fellow golfers, who tend to sting you even if your moustache flickers in the wind while they are putting.)

Bees have a mesh-like arrangement in their eyes, which can sense movement but cannot differentiate between golfers and trees. Have you ever seen a bee go for a tree as it goes for a golfer? The trick is to freeze if they are hovering overhead or even if they are in the near vicinity. Because distance is very misleading as far as bees are concerned. Again, Rambo-like heroism has absolutely no value here. We are talking about bees, man! You just concentrate on freezing.

Have you ever noticed how bees unite against a common enemy or a victim? It makes very little difference to the pack if the whole lot of them have been hurt or not. No matter where the others are, they will still want to add to the misery of the guy who is being stung red and blue, or blue and black, whichever the case might be. These creatures, which God manufactured ever so lovingly on a bad day, do not attack in a group to begin with. In the beginning, one or two will start the process by stinging the golfer who has done nothing but take a swing. That sting deposits some fluid, and the rest of the gang homes onto the fragrance. It actually has to be the smell of it, because the pack gets riled up in real style. One wonders if it is an aphrodisiac of some sort. Because the bees are then intent on rape, no matter what one does to distract them.

Keeping bees in mind, one should add a bottle of aftershave lotion to the golf kit. If one doesn't have it, and if you have time on your side (which you usually don't), you should quickly rub some grass on the place where you have been nicked by the pioneer. This masks the odour of the fluid and helps in confusing the rest of the gang. If nothing else works, and the bees are really giving you the works, run for the nearest sprinkler and let the bees drown in their own misery.

A point of observation here, which could help your AH factor from working overtime, is the flight patterns

Bees in battle mode.

of the bees. While on the ground, take a peek at their flight pattern. If it includes circular flying, it means that some of them are socialising, asking each other questions like "Hey baby! Where were you? Living in the same quarters and acting hard to get?" This attitude is fairly safe for they are on a routing flight. But if they seem to be flying in straight determined lines, then you better keep your head safely tucked in and be as inconspicuous as you can. A foetal posture will do very well. Best of luck anyway, but don't forget to see a doctor if you weren't lucky.

Golf and your Heart

Have you noticed that of all maladies affecting golfers on the course, including bee stings, snake bites, broken bones, split skulls, laceration, sand-in-the-eye situations, cerebral strokes, wry necks, back sprains, lightning strikes, injuries suffered when a golfer tries to literally burn the course, drowning in flash floods, mental trauma as a result of sexual abuse, monkey bites, alligator fear psychosis etc, the most frequent one is the heart attack or something related to the heart? This is because every one worries about snakes, bees, eagles carrying away your balls, or even dogs chasing you, but no one, as long as they can wallop the ball, ever gives their heart the consideration it requires.

Wrong attitude for those of us who are getting along in years! It becomes all the more essential to see where we are headed. These days, there is a distinct tendency to drink and smoke more, generally, but is more evident in younger golfers. Hence, direct and indirect afflictions of the heart tend to crop up earlier. If one has to do everything that one is not supposed to be doing, then at least some precautions are called for. Try to know about your risk factors. Here we would be talking about the family history of diabetes mellitis, early onset heart attacks or any young people in the family tree who suffered from cerebral strokes, the prevalence of hypertension, increased levels of cholesterol in other members etc. One should know about one's own blood pressure, blood biochemistry, and finally the electrocardiographic status. For golfers who are in the higher age group, getting a prophylactic Treadmill and Holter test is a good idea. You would be surprised to know what all happens to the heart during a period of 24 hours, while we are blissfully unaware of the on-goings. They certainly are a revelation. There is no sense in behaving like an ostrich.

When one has all this data under the belt, I am sure the level of confidence is much much higher when one belts the ball with good old lady Big Bertha. Mind you, this does not give anyone insurance against a heart attack. It can still come. But then, no one will blame you—you did your duty—to yourself and to you family.

A point of great importance arises when precordial discomfort comes on while one is actually playing golf. Here, a hypochondriac fares better than the others. Normal golfers suffer from a 'Denial syndrome.' They will attribute the pain to something that they have eaten or to their spondylosis. There are some who will carry the denial a step further by saying that "I can never get a heart attack. I can fly to the moon and back. This is just a stitch." When a renowned cardiologist suffered from chest pain while driving in the hills, he himself succumbed to the denial syndrome and paid with his life. The secret of the whole thing is to acknowledge the fact that the chest pain could be arising from the heart. The best thing would be sit or lie down, while one of your friends brings transport over to take you to the hospital. Let the doctor decide if the pain is from the heart or elsewhere. There is no shame involved. Even a sportsman can suffer a chest pain. Depending upon the results, one has to listen to the doctor for a change.

An interesting point came from the fertile mind of my good friend Sam Panwar, who suffered from a heart attack recently. What should the norm be if one of your four ball suffers a heart attack, say on 14th hole? Should play be suspended or the golfer dumped safely on the doctor's doorstep and play be resumed thereafter? Or should he be nicely tucked in on the edge of the rough, the caddy sent for transport while the other three finish the round? But a point of dispute could arise here. Should his partner be allowed to play two balls after adjusting shots according to his handicap minus his partner's? Or should his partner play his shot and drag, play shot and drag? This is fine but the round could take an awful lot of time! I suggest this aspect of the cardiac emergency be settled amicably lest some more golfers suffer heart attacks or physical trauma, should a riot erupt. For in India, lesser things have sparked riots.

Golfers should be given lessons in first aid, keeping such life threatening situations in mind. Especially mouth-to-mouth resuscitation, cardiac massage and Heimlich's procedure.

Heimlich's Procedure

Golfers are usually busy people. They have so many things to do. In order to fit their business or professional obligations into their golfing schedule, they have to be on their toes all the time. Mostly, their meals suffer the brunt of rescheduling. Quite a few times, one sees a golfer teeing off on a mouthful, bottle of Coca Cola in one hand and a sandwich in the other. If the ball departs on the intended course, things are fine. But if instead of drawing, there is a shank, then the mouthful may go down the wrong hatch—into the airway instead of the oesophagus. This is where the Heimlich procedure and knowledge of it comes handy.

In a nutshell, it should suffice to say that this is a life saving procedure to expel any foreign matter clogging the airway passage, because this space can never stand a foreign body in the first place. As a result, the lungs turn into airtight collapsible containers. The golfer, under these conditions, will be starved for air with surprising speed. His survival depends upon your speed if you are in the vicinity. He should be made to lie on the ground on his back, his head thrown back with the mouth wide open. Then the person performing the Heimlich procedure should press firmly just below the sternum with the heel of his right hand. The direction of the pressure should be upwards. This generates tremendous pressure inside the lungs and the foodstuff blocking the trachea is expelled with a whoosh. Believe me, this procedure has saved thousands of lives. Earlier, our forefathers would thump the poor fellow on the back. That *never* helped.

This procedure can come in handy at parties, or even when one is silly enough to get something lodged in the wrong places when one is all alone at home. In that case, just fall down on the arm of a sofa or the corner of a dining table, so that enough pressure is generated as explained. With a little presence of mind, one can even become a hero, by saving a life in one's lifetime.

The moral of the story—is Don't Get Too Emotional On a Mouthful. It could end up "Kitchi Mitchi......" Wrong hole. (I am sure you have heard of that).

Cardio-pulmonary Resuscitation

This important procedure should be known to all and sundry. Even the caddies and the waiters in the Gazebos. After all, these are out of bounds for the ball but not for a golfer who has an impending emergency crawling up his legs. It could hit him on the course, in the bathroom or in the rough. It doesn't really matter where. What matters is that the people who are in the vicinity of the incident should know what to do. It is usually the hapless golfer's four ball and his caddies who will be near him, if he is not in the habit of playing alone.

As you are about to hit your shot, you suddenly hear a loud thud and feel a faint tremor ascending up your club, and you turn to see the prostrate form behind you. You should feel his pulse and if there is none, then a mouth-to-mouth resuscitation is called for. No sense in hoping for a lady to try this on. Just tilt the guy's head and put your lips on his and blow, all the while closing his nostrils. Another person should be ready to do the cardiac massage. The proportion of mouth-to-mouth to cardiac massage should be 1:4.

The Paunch

Nearly all golfers have paunches, excepting the pros and the younger lot. The paunch adds to the dignity of the man concerned. A British study revealed that a small paunch was considered sexy. Thus, on the golf course, paunches can be categorised as sexy, average, not-so-sexy and the obscene. Apart from that, golfers should have a paunch which is convenient and which can support the elbows when one takes up a stance while addressing the ball. Such a paunch will deter wild swinging, acting as a fleshy obstacle.

It is a difficult job to maintain such a paunch, for paunches have a notorious tendency to increase. The following methods are suggested:

- A strict watch on your calories is a must. For this, one must count all the calories consumed.
- One must keep the mind off food and in-between eating.
- A regular routine of early morning exercising should be followed.

Alcohol and Golfers

Talking about paunches, alcohol contributes to the size of the paunch in a very positive way. Before I actually embark upon alcohol, let me tell you about the closely related 'cholesterol.' They have broken it up into further components, some of which have been called HDL, LDL and VLDL. Now, for the sake of simplicity, we can say that HDL is the good cholesterol, and the other two components are bad ones. They also say that alcohol and aerobic exercises increase the HDL and reduce the LDL and VLDL. *May I suggest, that planners of golf courses keep this fact in mind and plan courses in such a way that bars are placed at strategic places, so that golfers can play golf and jog from bar-to-bar-to-bar, thus keeping their cholesterol and paunch levels within reasonable levels?*

Golf is usually most disturbing, especially for those golfers who haven't read this book yet. The drives misbehave, the swing goes awry and trees decide to come in the way in almost every hole. The good golfer loses two balls and goes 'out-of-bounds' thrice, and finishes the round in one hundred and twenty! He then heads straight to the bar, to hit some birdies and eagles on the ninteenth. At least that brings down his score.

Golfing Dietetics

Obesity is an Eating Disorder!

Calorie restriction is the cornerstone of any weight reduction programme. The basic principles are simple: Essentially, the calorie supplied by protein, fat or carbohydrate has the same importance.

If calorie intake is less than calorie expenditure, stored calories, predominantly in the form of fat, will be consumed. In general, a 7,700 kcal deficit leads to a loss of 1 kilo fat only!

That large juicy apple you just ate gave you—

101 Calories

Now all that you have to do to burn those calories is:

Walk for	19 minutes
	Or
Ride the bike for	12 minutes
Swim for	9 minutes
	Or
Run for	5 mintues

Presto! The apple has been adequately looked after.

Mind you, these young golfers of today are in love with the colas and the pizzas along with soaked-in-oil-garlic bread. These people should remember that a medium sized pizza supplies about 1748 calories. Don't forget the garlic bread and the colas. One will really have to run from Chandigarh to Ambala and back to burn all those extra calories.

And after all the trouble you have gone through, if you still duff shots, hit duck hooks, bang trees which are miles from your line, miss two footers, then baby, all I can say is "At least we tried."

Reference Concentration Diversions

1. Mini novel by American poet Carl Sandburg:

   Pappa loved Mamma, Mamma loved men. Mamma's in the graveyard, Pappa's in the pen!

2. A golfing judge asks a boy in the witness box if he understood the nature of an oath. The lad replies, "Don't I? Aren't I your caddie?"

3. A beautiful girl in a diving suit comes up to a marooned golfer and asks him if he desires anything. The golfer says he would like some chocolate and cigarettes. The beauty pulls down a bit of her zipper and produces the chocolates and cigarettes. After the golfer has had them, she pulls her zipper down a bit more and with a twinkle in her eye, asks seductively, "Would you like to play around a bit?" The astonished golfer almost screams in ecstasy, "Holy Shit! You mean you have a full golf set in there?

4. Tom gets married and brings Jane home. They are both upset because the parrot passes embarrassing comments even if they come near each other. Despite Tom's threats, the

parrot doesn't stop. So Tom covers the cage with a towel and as a parting piece of advice, he tells the parrot that one more wisecrack will mean 'off-to-the-zoo' kind of a thing for him. The parrot gets the hint and is quiet. Meanwhile, Tom and Jane begin packing for their honeymoon. One overstuffed suitcase refuses to close. So Tom asks Jane to sit on it while he tries to close it. The parrot, with his vision obstructed, hears the following dialogue:

"Jane, darling, you come on top." After some time, "Tom, love, let's try by you coming on top." Meanwhile, the parrot hasn't forgotten the zoo threat. But when he hears, "Okay, let's both come on top!" he goes berserk and explodes, "Zoo or no zoo! This I gotta see for myself!"

5. A tired commuter reaches home to find his wife in bed with someone. He gets wild and very angry. Anyone would! He goes to the scoundrel and shouts, "Well, what the hell do you think you are doing?" The scoundrel replies that he is listening to music and quickly applies his ears to the lady's chest. The husband is confused and he also puts his ear to the lady's chest and declares, "Hell! I don't hear no music!" The scoundrel then quips, "Naturally! You do have to be plugged in, you know!"

6. Two simple women were walking on a street and they passed a hair saloon where hair treatment was being done. Consequently, a

whiff of burning hair reached the two simple women.

The first simple woman said, "Sniff, sniff! I say, Jane, do you smell burning hair?"

The second simple woman wondered, "Joan, do you think we are walking too fast?"

7. Two men died and met in heaven and got talking. It turned out that one was Santa Singh and the other was Banta Singh. To their surprise, both were from India, both used to lived in Chandigarh and on the same lane in Sector 26! Banta asked Santa, "Santaji, how did you die?"

   Santa replied with his head down, "I died of shame."

   "Shame? Why?"

   So Santa Singh told him how he thought his wife was having an affair with a fellow living on the same street. One day he was so sure he would catch them that he went home to surprise them. But he found no one. He was so ashamed of suspecting his wife that he died.

   "So, Banta Singhji, how did you die?"

   "Oh, I died of cold!"

   "How?" asked Santa Singh, "Chandigarh was never that cold."

   "You see, if you hadn't died of shame, you would have opened the refrigerator and caught me hiding there!"

8. The way some people play golf, the little green flags in holes should be at half-mast.

9. A golfer sliced a shot into a pig pen, killing one of the pigs. The irate owner lambasted the golfer who said, "I'll replace the pig!"

   "Forget it!" said the farmer, "you ain't fat enough!"

10. The gravestone proclaimed, "Here lies a lawyer and an honest man."

    A passerby said, "Can you imagine? Two people in the same grave?"

11. Jane died. When Harry was told about the tragedy, he exclaimed. "Oh Hell! I only hope she didn't die of anything serious!"

12. A blind man was standing at a crossroads when a dog came up to him and relieved himself along his trouser leg. To the astonishment of a passerby the blind man took out a biscuit and offered it to the dog. This so impressed the passerby that he went and complimented the blind man for his kindness to animals. The blind man retorted, "Kindness my foot! I was only trying to find out which side his mouth was, so that I could kick his other end!"

13. Bette Davis describing a young starlet with naked bitchiness, "There goes the good time that was had by all!"

14. A simple woman was asked which direction the elevator was travelling. She couldn't tell, even after she was given two guesses!

15. A fellow at a restaurant ordered a glass of warm grapefruit juice, two gooey eggs, burnt toast, cold coffee in a dirty cup with the rim chipped off. The waiter was taken aback and recovered sufficient wits to say that they don't make that kind of breakfast. To which the fellow replied, "Why not? You did it yesterday, didn't you?"

16. A salesman goes into a restaurant and tells the waitress to rustle up a breakfast of undrinkable coffee, burnt toast and gooey fried eggs. Then he tells the waitress to sit across him and nag him to near death. He says he has been on the road for so long that he is feeling homesick!

17. He is a real golf addict. Even his socks have eighteen holes.

18. Why don't you play with Harry anymore?" "Would you play with someone who moves the ball when you are not watching and enters the wrong score?"

    "No!"

    "Neither will Harry."

19. He doesn't cheat at golf. He plays for his health. And, of course, a low score makes him feel much better.

20. A caddie runs up to a golfer playing the Chandigarh course, "Good news is that you have a hole in one on the 5th. Bad news is that you are playing the fourteenth."

21. A divorcee was having an affair with a young stud. Elders from the locality approached her

and said, "Lady, we would like you to be a bit more discreet. Your activities are bad for the morals of our youngsters!" The lady appeared to be surprised. She denied the liaison and said, "As far as I am concerned, we have a 'platonic' relationship!" "Platonic, my foot!" shouted one elderly gentleman. "The stud visits you every night!"

"You see," replied the lady, "it is all 'PLAY' for him and a 'TONIC' for me!"

Many many thanks to my friends who contributed to my reference.